MW01634959

Gods & Goddesses

of Classical Mythology

GODS & GODDESSES

OF CLASSICAL MYTHOLOGY

SAMUEL WILLARD CROMPTON

Samuel Willard Crompton teaches history at Holyoke Community College. His love of mythology began when his mother, a novelist, read Greek and Roman stories aloud to him as a child.

Published by Grange Books
An Imprint of Grange Books PLC
Units 1–6, Industrial Estate
Hoo, near Rochester
Kent ME3 9ND

This edition published 1999

Produced in association with Saraband Inc.

ISBN: 1-84013-242-6

Printed in China

9 8 7 6 5 4 3 2 1

CONTENTS

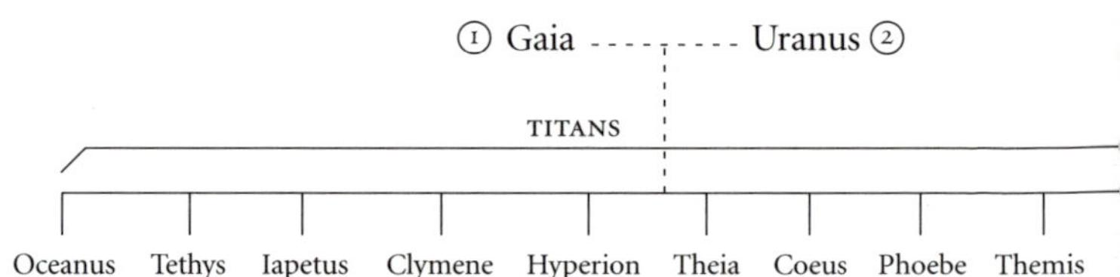

(1) Gaia
Uranus (2)
TITANS
Oceanus
Tethys
Iapetus
Clymene
Hyperion
Theia
Coeus
Phoebe
Themis

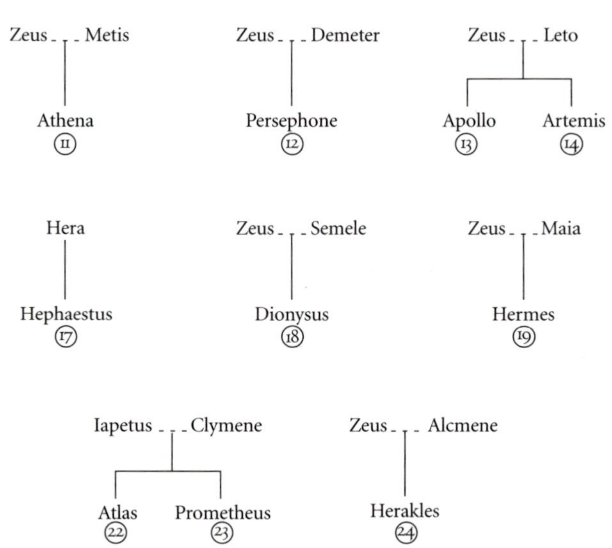

Zeus
Metis
Athena (11)
Zeus
Demeter
Persephone (12)
Zeus
Leto
Apollo (13)
Artemis (14)
Hera
Hephaestus (17)
Zeus
Semele
Dionysus (18)
Zeus
Maia
Hermes (19)
Iapetus
Clymene
Atlas (22)
Prometheus (23)
Zeus
Alcmene
Herakles (24)

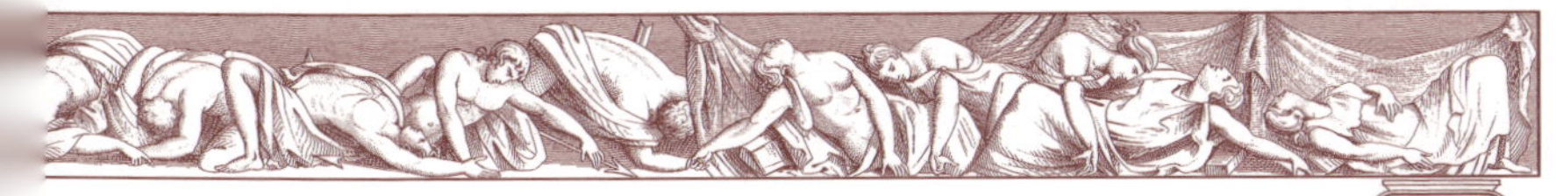

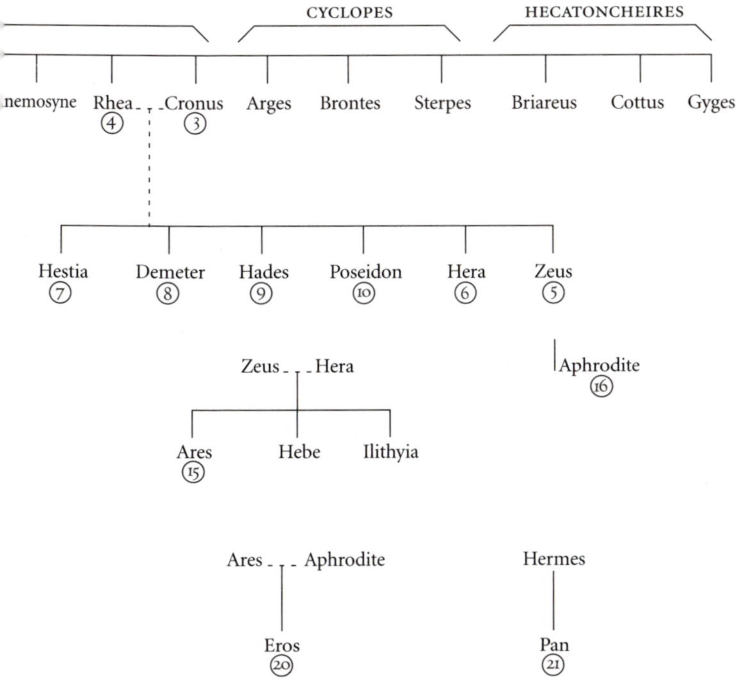

CYCLOPES

HECATONCHEIRES

[M]nemosyne — Rhea (4) - - - Cronus (3) — Arges — Brontes — Sterpes — Briareus — Cottus — Gyges

Hestia (7) — Demeter (8) — Hades (9) — Poseidon (10) — Hera (6) — Zeus (5)

Aphrodite (16)

Zeus - - - Hera

Ares (15) — Hebe — Ilithyia

Ares - - - Aphrodite

Eros (20)

Hermes

Pan (21)

INTRODUCTION

"As above, so below." The Greeks and Romans took this to mean that the gods and goddesses are very humanlike. From the flirtation and infatuation of Aphrodite to the rage and force of Ares, the gods express feelings and emotions that help us see aspects of ourselves within them. At the same time, humans demonstrate that they have some capacities that are godlike. Herakles's labors and the wanderings of Odysseus illustrate the tenacity and wisdom (as well as guile and cunning) that the ancient Greeks and Romans saw within themselves.

This anthropomorphic quality is seen in the songs of Homer (later codified in *The Iliad* and *The Odyssey*) and the poems of Hesiod (*Works and Days* and *Theogeny*). The Greek bards enshrined the lives and actions of a great number of immortals, ranging from the adolescent Adonis to mighty Zeus. In the stories of Homer and Hesiod, the Greeks emerge as human beings worthy of interplay and relationship with the gods. Since Greece and Rome are seen as the foundation of our modern Western world, it might be that the power and arrogance of European and American civilization grew out of the fact that the ancients saw themselves as, in some way, godlike.

It's important to see these deities of the past as living, breathing entities, not as pale visions of what the ancient peoples might have dreamed up. Let's see the classical divinities as they were portrayed: fanciful, vengeful, intensely emotional beings who watched the actions of humankind with interest and occasional disdain. Let us enter the mind and attitudes of Zeus, Hera, Apollo, Demeter and Persephone, and see in their lives and struggles the passions of our own hearts.

Turning to the stories of the gods and goddesses, we see that they are arranged in a family epic. The progression of rule is played out through the generational struggles of the gods of the Gold, Silver, Bronze, Heroic and Iron ages of man. The struggles for succession between Uranus and Cronus, then Cronus and Zeus, show that the Greeks (like the authors of soap-opera scripts) understood that the family story is the essential grist for the story of mankind.

Generations fight against each other, the Greek myths assert, and there is no way to escape the conflicts inherent in family life and civilization. To those who damn the Greek and Roman gods as hopelessly patriarchal, we might point to the figure of Gaia (Mother Earth) who begins the story of the gods and who helps the youngest sons (Cronus and Zeus) to overthrow their proud and cruel fathers.

Even as we recognize the sterling qualities of the Greek myths, we have to acknowledge that one important theme of

religion is absent from them. This is mercy. Zeus had Prometheus tortured daily for the sin of giving fire to humanity. Herakles killed people who "got in his way" almost indiscriminately during the course of his twelve labors. The Greeks sacked Troy with a vengeance and were themselves the victims of the rage of Poseidon and Athena after the war ended.

As we turn to look at the pantheon of Olympic Gods and their subordinate deities, let us imagine ourselves in the place of average Greek citizens and Roman subjects: people who toiled every day for a living, but who had a vision of the gods and goddesses that was both splendid and immediate. Gods were not far away and deaf; they attended to the human condition and were interested (though not often helpful) in the actions of mankind. Let us also be aware of the presence of the darker "shadow" emotions so often seen among the gods: envy, jealousy, fear and suspicion. The ancient Greeks, in their dramas and myths, allowed themselves to look at these shadow aspects in a manner that has never since been surpassed.

For consistency, we will use the Greek names of the gods in most cases (their Roman names appear in brackets). Exceptions include those Roman gods (Flora, Fauna, Janus, Carna and others) who do not have a Greek equivalent, and Diana, who is better known by her Roman name than by that of Artemis.

—SAMUEL WILLARD CROMPTON

I

MAJOR GODS & GODDESSES

The Family Saga

In the beginning there was **CHAOS.** The planets swirled and burned in darkness and the Earth sped through the galaxy. Born from this Chaos was **GAIA** (1), first of all the gods. Gaia was the Earth herself, but the planet was unformed when she first appeared. Gaia breathed life into the void and spread out her arms and legs, thereby creating rivers, mountains, streams and plains. As she became more fully developed, Gaia yearned for both a mate and children. She gave birth first to Uranus, the Sky, who then became her consort and lover.

The divine couple had three sets of children, known as the Titans, Cyclopes and Hecatoncheires. First came the twelve Titans, the youngest of whom was Cronus [Saturn]. Then Gaia bore the three Cyclopes: Arges, Brontes and Sterpes. Finally, she birthed the three Hecatoncheires: Briareus, Cottus and Gyges. Uranus feared the size and strength of his children, who derived their primal strength from their mother. He locked them in Tartarus, the deep underworld, to keep himself safe from them. Furious over the containment of her children, Gaia descended to the Underworld and persuaded her youngest Titan child, Cronus, to rebel against his father. Gaia provided the scythe with which Cronus castrated his father; the dripping blood from Uranus's genitals fertilized Gaia yet again and she gave birth to the Furies, Giants and Meliads (nymphs of ash trees).

Gaia presided over the marriage and family life of her children Cronus and Rhea [Ops], but when Cronus proved to be

a tyrant like his father, she helped Rhea to conceal the infant Zeus [Jupiter]. Zeus overthrew his father, as Cronus had Uranus, and then chained the other Titans in Tartarus.

Grieving over this, the second imprisonment of her progeny, Gaia mated with Tartarus (the Underworld) and gave birth to the many-headed monster Typhon, whom she sent forth against Zeus. The struggles were fierce, but Zeus prevailed; he buried Typhon under the volcano at Aetna, in Sicily. Thus the Titans and other children of Gaia remained subordinate to the new Olympian gods and goddesses. Gaia herself remained in the background, the ultimate Earth Mother, but no longer the object of direct worship by the Greeks. In her loyalty to her children and her assistance to Cronus and Zeus in the overthrow of their fathers, she is one of the most primitive and elemental of the Greek divinities. Almost forgotten by later generations, she set the whole epic of the gods in motion.

❁ **URANUS** (2) came directly from the womb of Gaia, her first-born. It is unclear how long his maturation took, but he became the lover and consort of his mother. In this role, Uranus was distinctly the junior partner of Gaia, and he feared the appearance of her children, who might dwarf him in size and strength. As each of their twelve children was born, Uranus chained them in Tartarus, the deep Underworld. Presiding

from above, he covered his ears so he might avoid hearing the screams of his children from their prison.

Uranus continued to consort with Gaia, but he had lost her love. She deceived him by giving a scythe to Cronus, their youngest child. As Uranus descended again to make love with his former mother and present wife, he was attacked and castrated by Cronus, wielding the scythe. The blood from his genitals fertilized Gaia once more and she gave birth to the Giants, Furies and nymphs of ash trees. Uranus withdrew immediately from the life of the gods and goddesses. It is unclear whether he ceased to have any power, but he cast a curse upon his son, swearing that Cronus should suffer the same fate—that one of his sons would revolt and dethrone him. Uranus disappeared from the Greek cosmology after he delivered his curse.

❁ **CRONUS** (3) [Saturn] *(pictured opposite)* was the twelfth child of Gaia and Uranus. Youngest of the brood of Titans, he nevertheless proved to have the greatest resolve. When Gaia, his mother, appeared to encourage her children to revolt against Uranus, it was Cronus who came forward and accepted her gift of a scythe with which to attack his father. Cronus waited patiently at the bedside of his mother and when Uranus appeared to make love, Cronus attacked and castrated him.

Having supplanted Uranus, Cronus freed his eleven siblings from their confinement in Tartarus. Grateful for his heroic work,

they agreed to be ruled by him, and Cronus apportioned to each of them some share of his domain. There followed a time in which Cronus ruled wisely and well: this was known to the Greeks as the Golden Age of Mankind, a time when people did not suffer from sickness or disease, and fertility reigned throughout the planet.

However, the curse that Uranus had passed down haunted Cronus, and as each of his own children appeared, he devoured them, to avoid being supplanted by a stronger offspring. Rhea, his sister and wife, watched with dismay as Cronus swallowed Hestia, Demeter, Hera, Hades and Poseidon. Seeking counsel from the Earth Mother, Gaia, Rhea concealed her sixth child, the baby Zeus, and gave his father a stone wrapped in cloth. Cronus devoured the package and forgot about Zeus, whom Rhea sent to the island of Crete for safekeeping.

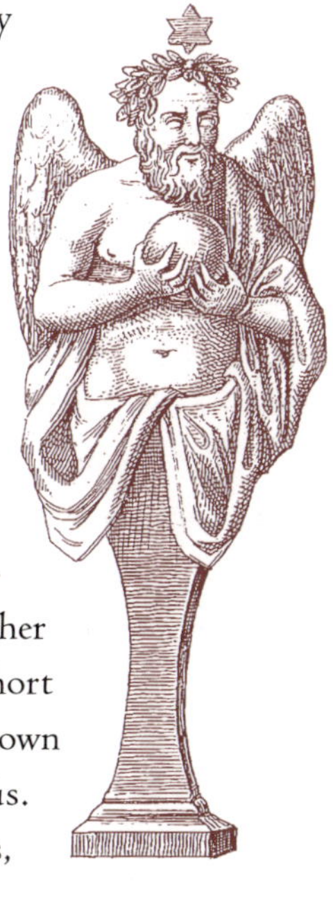

Later, Cronus was appalled to discover the existence of Zeus, and the father and son soon came to blows. After a short but terrible battle, Cronus was overthrown and exiled from Mount Olympus. Counseled by his first consort, Metis,

Zeus forced Cronus to take an emetic and disgorge the five children he had swallowed. Cronus retired to Italy and presided there as the Roman god Saturn, ruling wisely and well as a chastened lawgiver.

❁ **RHEA** (4) [Ops] was one of the Titans born to Gaia and Uranus. She was confined to Tartarus with her siblings until Cronus overthrew their father and freed them. Cronus and Rhea married and ruled from Mount Olympus as King and Queen of the world. Rhea gave birth to six children: Hestia, Demeter, Hera, Hades, Poseidon and Zeus. She watched with horror as Cronus devoured the first five children. Following the advice of the Earth Mother, Gaia, she managed to conceal and remove the baby Zeus from his father. Rhea sent Zeus to the island of Crete, where he was raised by nymphs and nursed by the fairy goat Amaltheia. By doing so, she provided for the ascension of a new generation of gods and goddesses: the Olympians, led by Zeus.

❁ **ZEUS** (5) [Jupiter] was the sixth child of Cronus and Rhea, raised by the nymphs Adrsteia and Ida and suckled on the milk of the fairy goat Amaltheia on the island of Crete. He grew to adulthood in secrecy, lest his presence be detected by his father.

Once he had attained his full maturity, Zeus revealed himself to Cronus and engaged in a short but terrible battle that ended with the son's victory. Zeus banished Cronus from Greece, but still had to confront the wrath of several of his uncles and aunts: the Titans. Some of the Titans accepted Zeus's position, but others resisted and a prolonged war (called the "Titanomachia") lasted for ten years. It was waged in Thessaly, where Zeus and his fellow gods fought from Mount Olympus while the Titans occupied Mount Othrys. Zeus won only through the gift of thunderbolts, given to him by the Cyclops (children of Gaia, born after the Titans). Even then, Zeus had to confront an enormous monster sent against him by the Earth Mother Gaia. After defeating Typhon, Zeus set up his rule on Mount Olympus.

Zeus gave lordship of the oceans and the Underworld to his brothers, Poseidon [Neptune] and Hades [Pluto]. Zeus was supreme and the three shared sovereignty of the Earth.

The ruler of Olympus was extremely amorous. His first consort was Metis, one of the female Titans. Hearing a prophecy that Metis would give birth to a child stronger than himself, Zeus swallowed her. Not long afterward, he suffered from a terrible headache. Hephaestus [Vulcan] rescued Zeus by

cleaving his forehead: out came the goddess Athena [Minerva], fully grown and armed. Next Zeus chose the Titanide Themis as his lover; she bore the Hours and Fates. He moved on to Eurynome, who provided Olympus with the Graces. Far from being contented, Zeus consorted with his sister Demeter [Ceres], who gave birth to Persephone [Proserpina]. The Nine Muses were born through his association with Mnemosyne; Apollo [Phoebus] and Diana were the product of his affair with Leto. Zeus finally "settled down" in marriage with his sister Hera [Juno], who was jealous of his amorous career. The couple had three children: Ares, Ilithyia and Hebe.

Always the most powerful god, though not always the wisest, Zeus presided over a tempestuous group of gods and goddesses. One major example of conflict among the immortals occurred during the Trojan War, which pitted Apollo and Ares [Mars] on the Trojan side against Athena and Hera on the side of the Greeks. Even Zeus found it difficult to control fellow Olympians. He generally favored Athena over the rest of his children, but at last he had to step in and order all his fellow gods to refrain from interfering in the Trojan War.

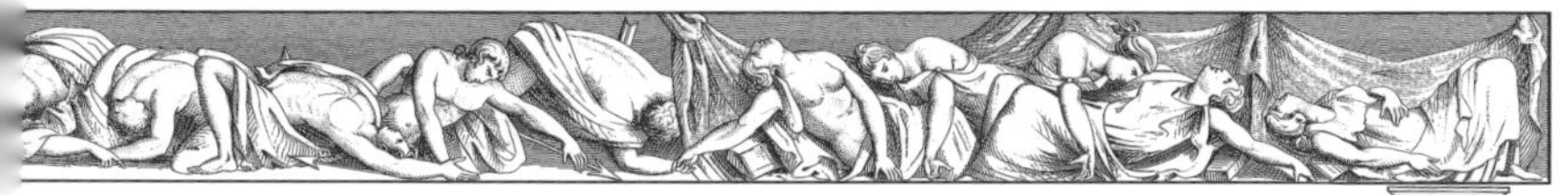

❁ **HERA** (6) [Juno] was the third child of Cronus and Rhea. Sheltered by one of the Titan couples during the war between Zeus and the Titans, she finally moved into a place of honor on Mount Olympus. She became the bride of Zeus, but was troubled by his seemingly endless affairs, both with goddesses and mortals. Hera's jealousy over these affairs knew no bounds. Hera gave birth to the god Hephaestus with no partner; in her marriage with Zeus she bore Ares, Ilithyia and Hebe.

After both Hera and Athena were slighted by the Trojan prince Paris, who judged Aphrodite [Venus] the most beautiful in a contest, the vain Hera swore vengeance against Paris and his city of Troy. During the Trojan War, she worked on behalf of the Greek invaders, drawing the wrath of her husband. Seen alternately as a shrew or as the protector of marriage and childbirth, Hera was an ambiguous figure. Mythologists see her jealousy and spitefulness as part of a general distrust of female behavior on the part of the Greeks.

❁ **HESTIA** (7) [Hesta] was the oldest of the six children born to Cronus and Rhea. After Zeus set up his rule on Olympus, Hestia became the goddess of fire, the household and home. The hearth was the center of the home, and both Greeks and Romans took care to worship Hestia, so that the vital core of their domestic life might never be extinguished. She was the gentlest of the Greek gods and goddesses.

DEMETER (8) [Ceres] was the second of the six children of Cronus and Rhea. The goddess of fertility and harvest, she was often referred to as the corn-goddess. As such she guarded the crops of Greece. Special altars were built to invoke her, especially in Attica, which required her protection for vineyards. Demeter was the second consort of Zeus. She gave birth to Persephone, and the separation of mother and daughter brought about the division of the year into the seasons of summer and winter.

HADES (9) [Pluto] was the first of three sons born to Cronus and Rhea. Like Hestia, Demeter, Poseidon and Hera, he had been swallowed by his father and then regurgitated. As the oldest of the three brothers, Hades received a place of honor and distinction: that of Lord of the Underworld. He ruled from a throne set deep below the Earth, where he welcomed the dead. Though he was a god of great power, said to possess all the mineral wealth of the Earth, the Greeks feared him and spoke as little as they could of him and his realm. The cypress tree and the narcissus were sacred to him.

POSEIDON (10) [Neptune] was the fourth child of Cronus and Rhea. After Zeus set up his rule on Mount Olympus, Poseidon received the oceans and rivers as his special domain. There he could rule as he saw fit. Even Zeus could not command Poseidon to do his bidding when it came to the tides and waves. Still, Poseidon was careful to seek agreement with Zeus and not to contest the overlordship of the heavens. The Greeks saw Poseidon as a moody god, one who supported the Greeks during the Trojan War, but then turned against Odysseus and hindered the hero's return to his home after the war ended. Poseidon was also known as the god and guardian of horses and the force that caused earthquakes. The Greeks also called him "Earth-shaker" and "Earth-girdler."

❁ **ATHENA** (II) [Minerva] was the daughter of Zeus and Metis, Greek goddess of prudence and a child of the Titans. When Metis became pregnant, she prophesied to Zeus that she would bear two children, the second of whom would be wiser and stronger than Zeus himself. In the manner of his father Cronus, Zeus swallowed his wife whole. Soon afterward, Zeus came down with a splitting headache, which no other god could cure. Turning to Hera's son, Hephaestus, Zeus asked him to split his head open. When Hephaestus did so, Athena, the daughter of Zeus and Metis, came forth, both armed and fully grown.

Athena was the goddess of both wisdom and military strategy. A masterful planner, she sided with the Greeks during the Trojan War, and was instrumental in the Greek victory. The city of Athens took Athena as its special patron. Athena often conducted business for Zeus, her father, wearing his shield when she did so. Despite her beauty and glory, Athena never married. She was one of the three goddesses who remained virgins (Hestia and Diana were the others). She rendered powerful assistance to such Greek heroes as Perseus, Theseus, Odysseus and Herakles.

Athena was the most powerful of the Greek goddesses. Some scholars today conjecture that her masculine attributes (strategy and war) were added onto an earlier goddess type who embodied more feminine virtues. Clearly, she had a vengeful streak, as shown by her treatment of Medusa, one of the three Gorgons.

PERSEPHONE (12) [Proserpina] was the daughter of Demeter, Zeus's second consort. The goddess of vegetation, she frolicked in fields and orchards as a child. Her gaiety gave joy to her mother, who blessed the Earth with great fruitfulness. But the joyfulness and beauty of Persephone attracted Hades, Lord of the Underworld, who stole up on and kidnapped Persephone, bringing her underground to serve as his queen.

Demeter was grief-stricken at the disappearance of her beloved daughter. She searched the whole Earth, but found no trace of Persephone. During this period, Demeter became an old woman and refused to do her duties as the fertility goddess. Plants shriveled and the harvest suffered greatly. When she learned that Hades had taken her daughter, Demeter went to Zeus and begged the chief god to release Persephone from Hades. Needing Demeter's help to fertilize the Earth, Zeus agreed. But when Hermes [Mercury] sped to the Underworld to free Persephone, it was found that she had eaten six seeds of pomegranate. According to the law of the Underworld, she had eaten the food of the dead and could not return entirely to the upper world. Hades decreed that Persephone might return to the surface for six months of the year, but she had to spend the other six months in Hades. Even Zeus was powerless to change the laws that governed Heaven, Earth and the Underworld. While Persephone remained in the Underworld, winter ruled the earth. When she came to visit Demeter, summer came with her.

❁ **APOLLO** (13) [Phoebus] was the son of Zeus and Leto, daughter of the Titan Coeus. Impregnated by Zeus, Leto went to Delos (one of the small Cycladian Islands in the strait between Rheneai and Myconos), where she bore twins: Apollo and Artemis [Diana]. Apollo was the god of healing, expiation and oracles. The arrows he carried in his quiver could bring sickness and death to mortals.

Portrayed in sculpture and art as a handsome, manly youth, Apollo carried either a bow or a lyre. In addition to his other concerns, he was the god of light. Each day, he drove his chariot across the sky dragging the sun. One of the great loves of Apollo's life was the nymph Daphne, who fled from his amorous approaches. Apollo pursued her, but upon catching up, found that his intended beloved had been changed into a laurel tree by her father, a river god. Apollo came away chastened by the experience; from that time on the laurel was sacred to him, and it served to commemorate victory in athletics and war. He favored the Trojans during their war with the Greeks.

Apollo's shrine at Delphi became renowned as the greatest oracle in ancient Greece. Delphi is situated in the narrow vale of the Pleistus, shut in by mountains on all sides.

❁ **DIANA** (14) was the twin sister of Apollo, daughter of Zeus and Leto. When she was introduced into the society of gods on Mount Olympus, she was deluged with requests for her hand in marriage. Diana went to her father Zeus and asked if she could remain single, a huntress, living in the woods. Zeus reluctantly concurred, and Diana became the symbol of the free female god.

Each evening, Diana mounted her moon chariot and drove across the heavens. Seeing the beautiful shepherd Endymion asleep, she marveled at his face, and sometimes bent down to kiss him. After the night journey was over, she took her bow and arrow and, accompanied by her maidens (all of whom were virgins), went into the woods to hunt for wild beasts. Although she was beautiful, Diana had a cool heart and she could, like her brother, be terrifying in anger. Her arrows caused swift and sudden death to those who opposed her.

❁ **ARES** (15) [Mars] was the first child of Zeus and Hera. Born into a family troubled by his father's infidelity, his love of strife is perhaps understandable. Tall and handsome, he was nonetheless the least liked of the gods, both by his fellow Olympians and by the Greeks, who feared him. The one true love of his life was Aphrodite, with whom he produced many children, even though Aphrodite was married to the god Hephaestus.

Large and strong in build, Ares was deficient in strategy and caution. Once his martial blood was stirred, he would throw himself heedlessly into the fray, which brought him into serious trouble on several occasions. He was captured by two Giants and imprisoned for thirteen months before being rescued by Hermes. He also appeared on the battlefield at Troy, where he was wounded by Diomedes. Ares repaired quickly to Mount Olympus and complained to Zeus, who ordered him to stay out of the Trojan War. Ares was also jealous of the successes of the hero Herakles [Hercules], whom he appeared to fight on two occasions (at Pylos and in defense of his son, Cycnus). He was wounded twice. No one can tell if Ares would have overcome the mortal, since Zeus separated the two with a thunderbolt.

Generally disliked because of his predilection for war and bloodshed, Ares represented the power of elemental, barbaric warfare to the Greeks. Although they respected his martial spirit, which encouraged them to resist and defeat Persia, they generally preferred the wisdom and strategy of Athena.

❁ **APHRODITE** (16) [Venus] was the goddess of love. Her parentage is uncertain: some accounts link her birth to an association between Zeus and Dione; others say she came from the water fertilized by the genitals of Uranus when he was castrated by Cronus. She was first seen by the West Wind, which watched her rise out of the sea on a cushion of foam at dawn. The three Graces became her attendants. Zeus never publicly acknowledged Aphrodite as his daughter, but he welcomed her to Mount Olympus, where she reigned as the least warlike of the gods and goddesses. One of her most important moments came when the Trojan prince Paris awarded her the prize for beauty over Hera and Athena. Aphrodite remained devoted to Paris and worked on his side during the Trojan War.

Knowing that her beauty would cause dissension among the gods, Zeus married Aphrodite to Hephaestus, the most gentle and kind of the Greek gods but also the homeliest. Like most of the goddesses, she was an unfaithful wife and consorted with Ares, the god of war. Once a year she returned to Cythera, an island off southern Greece, and dived into the sea from which she had come. Each time she rose as young and radiant as before.

❁ **HEPHAESTUS** (17) [Vulcan] was the god of fire, smiths and crafts. He was born of Hera alone, without a father. Very fond of his mother, he sometimes sided with her in arguments against Zeus. Once, infuriated by Hephaestus's words, Zeus grabbed the god and threw him headlong out of Mount Olympus. He fell all day and landed on the island of Lemnos (in the Aegean Sea, midway between Mount Athos and the Hellespont), laming his legs in the fall. Although he was welcomed back to the company of the gods later, Hephaestus remained in the shadows at Mount Olympus. Extremely gentle and forebearing, he worked at his crafts and was worshipped by the Greeks as the master of the arts of fire and smithing.

Hephaestus was married to the goddess Aphrodite soon after she arrived on Olympus. Learning of her affair with Ares, he sneaked up on the lovers and entangled them in a net to be brought before the other immortals. The lovers were deeply shamed, but this action did not make Aphrodite a faithful wife.

Hephaestus built two robots of gold that served to help him walk. He also made the twelve golden thrones of the gods in his workshop on Olympus. Known for devotion to his craft and personal kindness, he was one of the most sympathetic of the Olympian gods.

❁ **DIONYSUS** (18) [Bacchus] was the son of Zeus and the mortal Semele. As usual, Zeus conducted his affair in secret; as usual, Hera found out about the match. She tempted Semele into asking Zeus to reveal himself to her in his full glory. Semele lured the foremost god into swearing an oath by the River Styx that he would fulfill her one wish. To his great sorrow, she asked him to show himself to her fully: Semele died as a result. Dionysus, the youngest of the major gods of Olympus, was raised by the Maenads, nymphs who lived in the valley of Nysa. Hera resisted his coming to Olympus, but Zeus insisted. When Dionysus arrived, there were only twelve golden thrones. The modest goddess Hestia rose and offered her throne to Dionysus, saying that there was no need for her to sit, since her task was to keep the household fire burning.

Dionysus created the wine that became a sacred pleasure to both the Greeks and the Romans. He caused milk and honey to flow from nature. In the form of a goat or a bull (both symbols were signs of fertility), he created a secret cult, or following, of maidens who lost themselves in the tumult of orgiastic pleasure. The cult of Dionysus was close in spirit to the worship of Demeter.

Adult male Greeks generally chose to ally themselves with either Dionysus or Apollo. Those who chose Dionysus emphasized pleasure and virility, while those who admired Apollo sought honor for their logic or artistic accomplishments.

❂ **HERMES** (19) [Mercury] was the son of Zeus and Maia, a nymph from the Titans' era. She and Zeus married in secret, and Hermes was born on Mount Cyllene in Arcadia. Mischievous from the very beginning, Hermes stole a herd of cattle from his half-brother Apollo while he was still a babe. Apollo chased him down and brought him to Olympus, where Hermes gave the lyre that he had invented to mitigate his brother's anger.

Hermes became the trusted messenger of the gods, and of Zeus in particular. To speed his travels, Zeus equipped him with winged sandals (the Talaria) and a winged cap (the Petasus). The protector of tradesmen and travelers, Hermes was also the patron of liars and thieves (although he himself never lied again after his deceit of Apollo). He had the honor of leading the souls of the dead into the afterlife. His festivals in Rome were held in the month of May, derived from his Roman name, Mercury. The number four was sacred to him, as he was born on that date.

❂ **EROS** (20) [Cupid] was the son of Ares and Aphrodite. Shown as a beautiful winged boy equipped with bow and quiver, he shot his arrows in a way that inflamed the hearts of both gods and men. Even Zeus was not immune to his arrows, and Eros was himself struck with love for Psyche. He was known for fostering friendship between men and boys, and the Spartans paid homage to him before battle. Eros carried out missions for his mother, the love goddess.

PAN (21) [Faunus] was the son of Hermes; the myths name different mothers (including a goat). When he was brought to Mount Olympus by his father, the other gods laughed because he was quite homely. Portrayed as having the horns and legs of a male goat, he was hale and hearty but quite unsociable. The gods named him Pan and sent him back into the world to act as the god of the fields and woods. The Greek god of Nature, Pan would usually appear suddenly and startle all the humans and animals around, giving rise to the word "panic." He lived in a cave and usually appeared outside in the midday heat. A god of vegetation, Pan was notable for his solitary habits. His importance has often been obscured by his poor public image. He stood for all that was wild and untamed in the world, indeed, all that was not human. He was the patron of drama, music and intoxication, and the tortoise was sacred to him.

❁ **ATLAS** (22) was a son of the Titan Iapetus and a brother of Prometheus. He took part in the war between the Titans and the gods on the Titan side. When the war ended, Zeus punished him by making him carry the vault of heaven—the sky—on his shoulders. There he stood, shoulders and arms aching, for what must have seemed an eternity.

Atlas drew some comfort from the prophecy that two sons of Zeus would come his way eventually (he hoped one of them might relieve him of his burden). Herakles was the first: he stole the golden apples of the Hesperides, but failed to help Atlas. The task then fell to Perseus, who, after he slew the Gorgon Medusa, passed Atlas as he was flying back to Greece. Atlas begged the hero to show him the dreaded face of Medusa, which turned viewers to stone, so he might be freed from his burden. Perseus obliged, and Atlas was frozen into stone, thereby creating the Atlas mountain range of northwest Africa.

PROMETHEUS (23) was a son of the Titan Iapetus and a brother of Atlas. Although he did not fight against Zeus in the war between the gods and the Titans, he had no love for the new world order created by the rulers of Mount Olympus. Some sources tell us that Prometheus (whose name means "he who thinks in advance") was given power to create the first men and women out of clay. Whether or not this was true, he nourished a love for mankind and asked Zeus to give fire to the first humans. Zeus curtly refused: fire was to be a tool for the gods alone. Prometheus took a glowing ember from the sacred fire of Olympus, concealed it in a hollow stalk of fennel and brought it down from heaven as his gift to mankind, thereby changing the course of human history.

Zeus was furious over the deceit. He ordered that Prometheus be chained to the top of the Caucasus Mountains (in present-day Georgia). Every day an eagle would swoop down and tear at Prometheus's liver until it was nearly destroyed. At night the liver would regenerate itself, and the eagle would

return the next day and resume the awful cycle that kept Prometheus in perpetual agony. It was told that Prometheus endured this suffering for some 1,000 years.

Prometheus was finally freed by the hero Herakles, who shot the eagle with an arrow. Herakles arranged a bargain by which Prometheus could go free and remain immortal, while the Centaur Cheiron would give up his own immortality, which caused him great pain because of a wound that could not be healed. Prometheus returned to Olympus and reassumed his role of counsel to the gods.

HERAKLES (24) [Hercules] was the greatest hero of Greece and the only human to earn his way to immortality. He was the son of Zeus and the mortal Alcmene. Zeus fathered Herakles to create a human hero capable of fighting with the Olympian gods in their coming battle against the Giants.

Jealous, as usual, of her husband's amours, Hera sent two serpents to kill the infant Herakles, but he strangled the snakes. Growing to manhood, Herakles was recognized everywhere as the strongest human being. His success in life seemed certain until he aroused the anger of Hera again, when she sent Lyssa (the daemon of madness) to him. He became temporarily insane and, in his rage, killed his own wife and children. To atone for this, he found he had to perform twelve heroic labors for his cousin, King Eurystheus of Tiryns.

The twelve labors were as follows. Herakles killed the Nemean Lion (1) and the Hydra (2). He captured the Cerynitian hind (a stag with golden horns that was sacred to Artemis) (3) and took the Erymanthian boar alive (4). He cleaned the filthy stables of Aegeas, the king of Ellis, by diverting a river to wash through them (5) and chased away the Stymphalian birds (6). Herakles then captured the Cretan bull and brought it to King Eurystheus (7) and fetched the man-eating mares of Diomedes, the king of Thrace (8). He went to the land of the Amazons and took the magic belt of their queen, Hippolyta (9). He brought the cattle of King Geryon of Erytheia (10) and stole the golden apples of Hera from the Hesperides (11). His last and most formidable task was to capture and bring Cerberus, the three-headed hound of Hell, into the light of day. Terrified by the appearance of the monster, King Eurystheus had Herakles return Cerberus to Hades.

Herakles's exploits aroused the wrath and envy of both gods and men. He fought and wounded

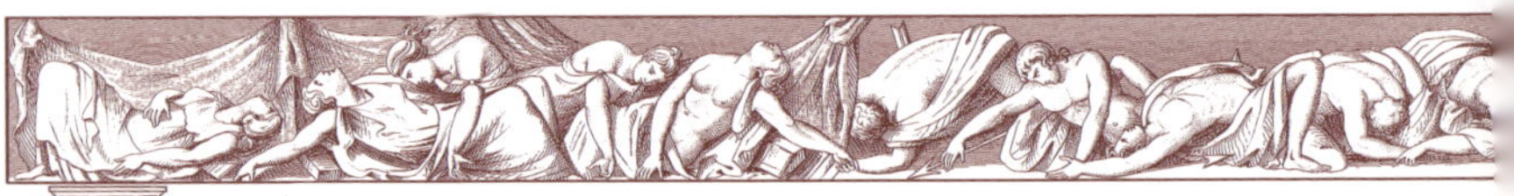

Hades, Hera and Ares and took revenge on men who had deceived him, including the leaders of Troy and Pylos. Fated to fall at the hands of trickery, Herakles fatally wounded the Centaur Nessus with one of his arrows. In his dying moments, the Centaur gave a poisonous potion to Herakles's second wife, Deianira, saying that it would keep the hero in love with her. Years later, she rubbed the mixture into a cloak and gave it to her husband. The cloak brought Herakles close to death, whereupon he built a funeral pyre on Mount Oite in Thessaly. Herakles mounted the pyre, resigned to death. But Zeus sent thunder and lightning to bring the hero to Mount Olympus and gave him a place among the immortals.

His services were soon needed there as well. War between the Olympian gods and the Giants was impending, and many of the Giants could only be killed by the poisoned arrows of Herakles. He was reconciled with Hera, who gave her daughter Hebe to be his wife, and Herakles assumed the pleasant task of gatekeeper of Olympus.

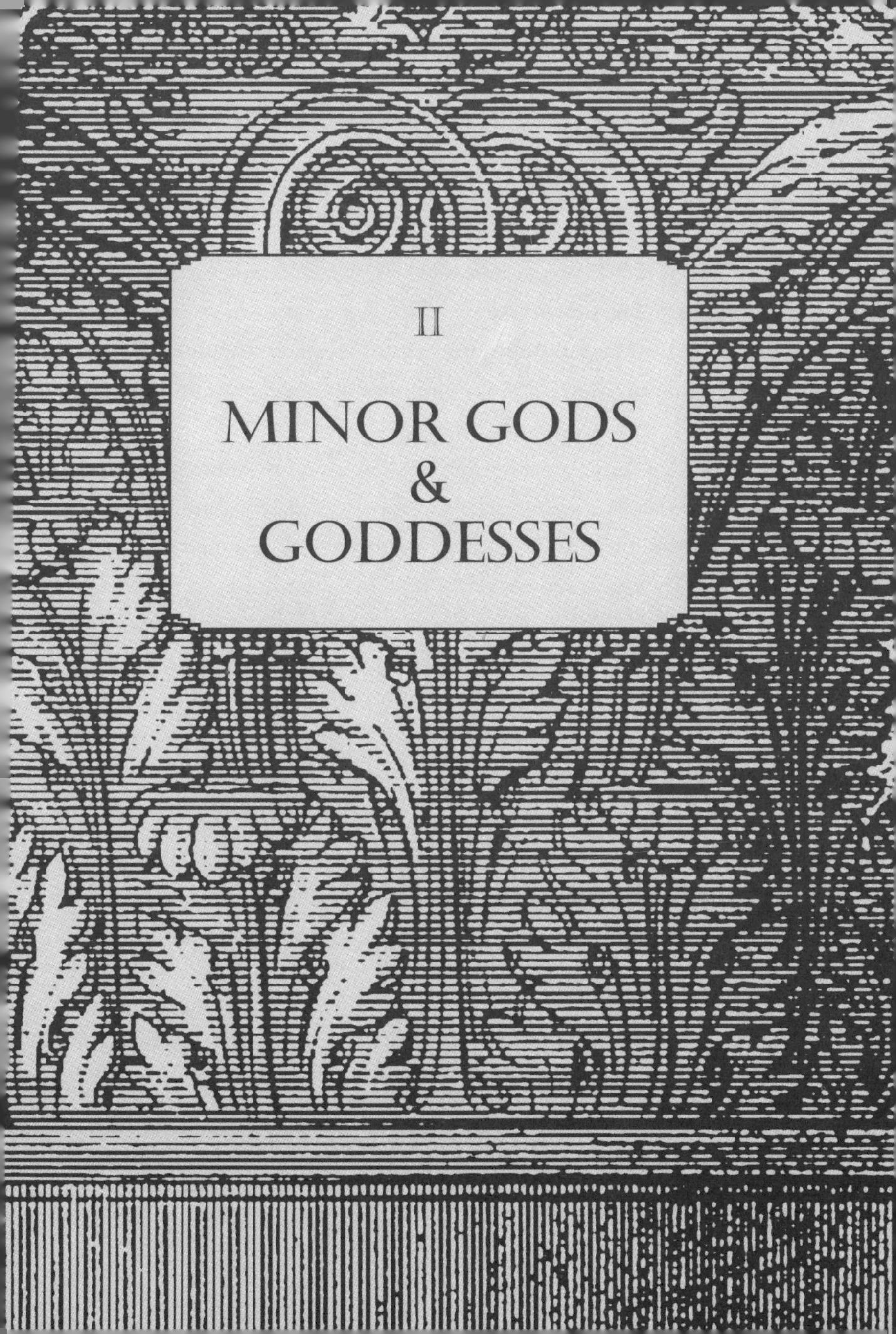

II

MINOR GODS & GODDESSES

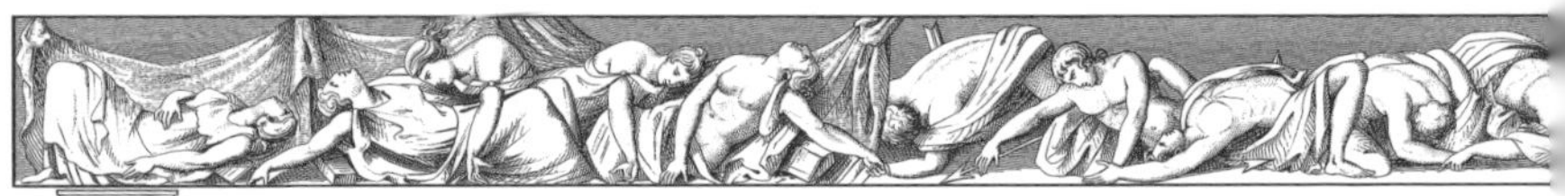

ADONIS was a beautiful youth with whom Aphrodite fell in love and had two children. When Adonis was killed while hunting a wild boar, Aphrodite grieved so much that Zeus allowed Adonis to return from the Underworld for a portion of each year.

ASCLEPIUS was a son of Apollo and the mortal Coronis, raised and tutored by Cheiron, the wise Centaur. Asclepius came to rival and even surpass his father in the healing arts. He had a wife and seven children, one of whom was Hygeia. After Asclepius tried to bring the dead back to life, Zeus struck him down with a thunderbolt, angry that a mortal being should aspire to such power.

AURORA was the Roman goddess of the dawn (her Greek name was Eos). She was pictured rising from the ocean in a chariot. The sister of Helios and Selene, she married Astraeus and was the mother of the four winds: Boreas (north), Eosphorus (east), Notus (south), and Zephyrus (west).

BOREAS *(pictured at right)* was the god of the north wind. The Athenians revered him, especially after a Persian invasion fleet was wrecked in a storm off the Greek coast. He was represented as a scowling, bearded old man.

❁ **CARNA** was a Roman goddess. A virgin, she tricked potential lovers into entering a cave with the promise that she would follow them, then promptly vanished. The only being to make love with her was the Roman god Janus, who gave her power over homes and doorways. She was also the guardian of physical health, especially the internal organs: heart, lungs and liver. *Caro* meant flesh, hence the term "carnal." Her feast was celebrated on June 1.

❁ **CASTOR AND POLLUX** were brothers and Roman heroes, known as the Dioscuri, meaning sons of Zeus. The sons of Zeus and Leda, they were brothers to Helen and Clytemnestra (see TROJAN WAR). Castor was famed for taming and managing horses; Pollux was renowned for his boxing skill. The brothers embarked on three great adventures: an expedition against Athens, the voyage of the Argonauts in search of the Golden Fleece and their battle with the sons of Aphareus. Castor was killed in the last adventure, and Zeus gave Pollux the alternatives of being made immortal alone, or dividing his time between Castor in the Underworld and the gods on Olympus. Pollux chose the latter course, and the brothers retained their bond. Their Roman feast day was July 15.

❁ **CHARON** was the son of Nyx (Night) and Erebus. He had the task of ferrying the souls of the dead across the dreaded River Styx. Charon would only do so if the person had been buried properly and the relatives had placed a gold coin in the dead person's mouth, as Charon's fee. Those who had not received a proper burial were required to wander along the banks of the river for a hundred years to earn the right to cross.

❁ **CHEIRON** was the son of Cronus and Philyra. He was a Centaur (half man and half horse), but unlike most of his kind he was wise, gentle and learned. He tutored most of the great Greek heroes: Achilles, Herakles, Jason, Aeneas and Peleus. A tragedy occurred when Herakles accidentally wounded him in the groin with a flaming arrow while aiming at a group of riotous Centaurs whom Cheiron was seeking to control. Being immortal, but not invulnerable, Cheiron was thus condemned to suffer unbearable pain for eternity. Seeing a possible solution, he asked Zeus to exchange his immortality for the mortal pains of Prometheus. Zeus agreed and Cheiron died.

❁ **CLIO** was the first of the nine Muses, daughters of Zeus and Mnemosyne (Memory). She presided over History. Crowned with laurels, she was depicted holding a book and quill with which she recorded the acts of the Greek heroes (see THE MUSES for her eight sisters).

❁ **CONCORDIA** was a Roman goddess, the personification of harmony. The Romans dedicated shrines to her after major civil disputes had been settled, and the magistrates used her temple to transact public business. She was portrayed as a matronly woman who held an olive branch in her left hand and the cornucopia (horn of plenty) in her right.

❁ **DISCORDIA** was the Roman goddess of dissension and strife. Her Greek equivalent was Eris. The daughter of Nyx (Night), Discordia provided the spark that lit the flame of the Trojan War. At the marriage of Peleus and Thetis (to which she had not been invited), Discordia tossed an apple among the wedding guests inscribed "To the Fairest." This led to a competition among Aphrodite, Hera and Athena. After Prince Paris of Troy selected Aphrodite as the fairest, the stage was set for the abduction of Helen and the ten-year struggle between Greece and Troy.

❁ **ECHO** was a wood nymph whose duty was to attend Hera. Once, she prevented Hera from learning about one of Zeus's affairs by chattering loudly. Furious over the deceit, Hera punished the nymph by depriving her of normal speech: she could only repeat the last words that others had said. Echo later fell in love with Narcissus, the mortal who loved only his own reflection in the water. When he failed to return her affection, she pined and faded away, becoming nothing more than a distant echo.

❁ **EREBUS** was the primeval god of darkness, one of the children of Chaos. With his sister Nyx, he fathered Aether (the atmosphere), Hemera (Day) and Charon, the ferryman of the River Styx in Hades.

❁ **FAUNA** was a Roman goddess. She married Faunus, the Roman god of shepherds and the countryside (the equivalent of Pan). It is said that she never looked at another man after her marriage. Gifted with the power of prophecy, she had the power to bless the Roman farmers, and was therefore often called *Bona Dea* (good goddess). Some scholars suspect that this tribute was paid more out of fear than love of Fauna.

❁ **FLORA** *(pictured at left)* was the Roman goddess of flowers and springtime. She commanded the vegetative power that made trees blossom, and it was said that her breath became petals and her footprints, flowers. Her feast, the Floralia, was celebrated in Rome between April 28 and the beginning of May. Like its Celtic counterpart, Beltane, the Floralia was noted for excess in terms of drink and orgiastic sexual relations.

FORTUNA *(pictured at right)* was the Roman goddess associated with fortune and luck. Often depicted as blind, she was shown with a cornucopia (the horn of plenty) and a rudder (symbolizing her ability to turn the direction of human lives). After the Roman Republic was replaced by the empire, each emperor had his own personal "Fortuna" to guide him. Her festival, the Augustilia, was held October 3-12.

HEBE was the goddess who represented the freshness of youth. Daughter of Zeus and Hera, sister of Ares, she was the cupbearer of the other gods and goddesses. When Herakles was granted immortality, Hera gave him Hebe's hand in marriage. The couple had two children: Alexiares and Anicetus.

HELIOS was a Greek sun god who predated Apollo. One of the Titans, he was the son of Hyperion and Theia. Helios drove his chariot of fire across the sky each day, drawn by the legendary horses Pyrios, Eos, Aethon and Phlegon. The Colossus of Rhodes, one of the Seven Wonders of the Ancient World, was a statue of Helios.

❁ **HYGEIA** was the Greek goddess of health. One of the daughters of Asclepius, she was shown holding a cup of water in one hand and a snake in the other, which drank of the water.

❁ **HYMENAEUS** [Hymen] was the Greek god of marriage. One myth called him the son of Dionysus and Aphrodite. The second story held that he was a handsome Athenian youth, who, spurned by the young women of the city, turned his energy to rescuing them from grave danger when they went out to sea. As a result of his perseverance, he was rewarded with marriage to a beautiful maiden. Hymenaeus was depicted as a handsome youth with a bridal torch in one hand and a garland in the other.

❁ **HYPNOS** was the god of sleep. A son of Nyx (Night) and Erebus, he lived in a cave on the island of Lemnos. His importance to the other gods can be shown in an anecdote from the Trojan War. Eager to cast her influence on the side of the Greeks, Hera persuaded Hypnos to lull Zeus to sleep so that his brother Poseidon (who detested the Trojans) could intervene on behalf of the Greeks. The word "hypnosis" springs from this legend.

❁ **IRIS** was the goddess of the rainbow and (prior to Hermes) first messenger of the gods. She married Zephyrus, god of the west wind. Iris had the duty of cutting the thread that bound the souls of the dying to their bodies at the time of death.

JANUS *(pictured at left)* was a Roman god who had no counterpart in Greek mythology. He had two faces, looking either forward and backward, or east and west. The god of beginnings, gates and avenues, he was always the first to be evoked in Roman ritual. The doors of his temple in Rome were closed only in times of peace (which meant that they were usually open!) His tools were a set of keys and a janitor's staff. His festival, the Agonia, was celebrated on January 9.

KALYPSO was a Greek nymph who welcomed the shipwrecked Odysseus to her island of Ogygia in the western Mediterranean (some scholars associate it with the Moroccan peninsula of Ceuta). Kalypso kept Odysseus safe for seven years, begging him to marry her; in return she would grant him immortality. Fortified by advice from Athena, Odysseus held out for the seven years, until Zeus sent Hermes down to Ogygia to command that she release the hero. Kalypso did so reluctantly, but she gave Odysseus food and wood to make a raft, and showed him the stars by which to navigate his way.

LAVERNA was the Roman goddess of thieves and cheaters. Believed to protect all those who plot or deceive, she was very popular in Rome. Libations to her were poured from the left hand, which may account for some of the prejudice in the modern world against left-handed persons.

LETHE was the Greek goddess of oblivion and forgetfulness. A daughter of Eris (Discordia in Rome), she ruled one of the six rivers that flowed in Hades. The souls of the dead had to drink from the river Lethe, to forget their previous lives and be born anew.

LIBERTAS was the Roman god of freedom and liberty. She held a rod in one hand, a cap in the other, representing the rod that magistrates used to free slaves and the cap worn by such freedmen. Clearly, she was more a symbol of the Roman Republic than of the Roman Empire. She appears in much of the symbolic architecture of Washington, D.C., and was also an emblem of the French Revolution.

LIBITINA was a Roman goddess who supervised the rites on behalf of the souls of the dead. Her shrine was in a sacred wood south of Rome. Due to the close ties between their names, she was often confused with LIBIDO, an ancient Roman goddess of sexual passion.

❁ **LUNA** was the Roman goddess of the moon. She induced spells of madness in those who angered or offended her.

❁ **METIS** was the Greek goddess of prudence. A daughter of the Titans Oceanus and Tethys, she was the first consort of Zeus. After she prophesied that she would bear first a daughter and then a son who would rule the world, Zeus swallowed Metis. He soon came down with a tremendous headache and ordered Hephaestus to split his forehead open (perhaps originating the expression a "splitting headache"). Out jumped Athena, fully grown and armed. Metis was no more, but her prudence had been passed on to Athena, who became the goddess of wisdom.

❁ **MOMUS** was the Greek god of blame, sarcasm and satire. A son of Nyx (Night), he was known for his carping criticism of every other god, goddess and situation. He even managed to find fault with Aphrodite, claiming her footsteps were too loud for such a dainty goddess. After Gaia declared that the human population was growing too large, Momus suggested the Theban and Trojan Wars as an antidote. Finally, the gods drove him from Olympus.

❁ **MORPHEUS** was the Greek god of dreams. A son of Hypnos, he was the sender of visions to mankind. The drug morphine was named after him by the German chemist F.W.A. Serturner, in 1806.

❁ **NEMESIS** was the Greek goddess of balance and retribution. A daughter of Nyx and Erebus, she saw to it that good and bad luck were almost evenly divided in the lives of human beings. As such, she provided an important counterweight to the goddess Fortuna, who had the power only to bless.

❁ **NIKE** was a Greek goddess, the personification of victory. One of the daughters of Styx, she supported the Olympian gods in the great war between Zeus and Cronus. A winged messenger, she attended Athena. Nike held a palm branch in one hand and a garland in the other.

❁ **NYX** was the primeval goddess of night, one of the children of Chaos. She mated with Erebus and gave birth to Hypnos, Thanatos, Momus, Nemesis, Aeleus, the Hesperides and the Fates.

❁ **PAX** was the divine representation of peace in Rome. After the ferocious civil wars of the first century BC (fought among Caesar and Pompey, Antony and Octavian), the victorious

Octavian, now Augustus, had an altar built to indicate the re-establishment of civil order. Later, the Emperor Vespasian devoted a temple in the Forum to Pax: the entire complex was renamed the "Forum of Peace."

❁ **PEGASUS**, a magical winged horse, was born of the blood that dropped when Medusa's head was cut off by Perseus. The Greek hero Bellerephon caught Pegasus and used the horse's great powers to defeat the Chimera, a fire-breathing monster that lived in Lycia. When the pair approached Olympus, Zeus unseated the hero and allowed only Pegasus to enter heaven, where he became one of the constellations.

❁ **PROTEUS** was a god of the sea who tended the flocks of seals and other sea creatures. He lived on the island of Pharos, close to the mouth of the Nile. Proteus could change into any shape he desired—animal or elemental force. He often did this to escape the relentless questions of humans, who came to him because he was known to have the gift of prophecy.

❁ **PSYCHE** (the Soul) was one of the three daughters of a Greek king. Her two sisters were fair to look upon, but she was beautiful beyond compare. Eros, the god of love, was smitten by his own arrows and fell completely in love with her. He brought her far away from her family and surrounded

her with affection and comfort, with only one proviso: that she should never look at him. The two made love each night in the dark.

Tempted by her two sisters, who were extremely jealous of her good fortune, Psyche finally dared to look on Eros with her lamp while he was sleeping and spilled a few drops of oil on him. He awoke immediately, understood that she had broken her word and fled to Olympus, where his mother Aphrodite tended to him.

Aphrodite laid numerous curses on Pysche, making her life utterly miserable. When Psyche gathered her nerve to approach Aphrodite, the goddess of love set enormous tasks for her. Finally, Eros came back to himself, found Psyche and persuaded Zeus to allow him to marry a mortal. It is unclear whether Psyche became a goddess herself as a result. If so, she was like Herakles: she had "earned" her way up in the world. Her story became the foundation for understanding the trials that the soul undergoes in its search for true love.

❁ **SOL** was the Roman sun god. A divinity of the Sabines, he was brought to Rome during the reign of King Titus Tatius, prior to the formation of the Roman Republic.

❁ **STYX** was the goddess of the River Styx, in Hades. One of the children of Nyx, she married Pallas and gave birth to Zelus, Nike, Cratus (Power) and Bia (Strength). She and her children supported Zeus in the great war between the Olympians and the Titans. As a reward, Zeus gave Styx the honor of being the greatest and surest oath any god could swear by. Even Zeus himself could not revoke an oath he had sworn "by the River Styx" (see the story of Semele under DIONYSUS).

❁ **TARTARUS** was one of the primeval elements, brought to life out of Chaos at the beginning of time. He was the Underworld itself. Tartarus was located as far below Hades as Hades was distant from the surface of the Earth.

❁ **TETHYS** was a primordial force that personified the fertility of the seas. A daughter of Uranus and Gaia, she married her brother Oceanus and gave birth to more than 3,000 children, who became the rivers and streams of the world. She brought up the young Hera during the great war between the Olympians and the Titans.

❁ **THANATOS** was a masculine winged spirit who personified Death. He was the brother of Hypnos (Sleep) and one of the sons of Nyx.

❁ **THEMIS** was another daughter of Uranus and Gaia. The goddess of eternal law, she was the second of the consorts of Zeus. Themis gave birth to the Hours and Fates (Horae and Moirai). Themis advised Zeus and taught Apollo the technique of prophecy. She was one of the few Titans and Titanides to be given a place of honor on Olympus.

❁ **VOLUPIA** was a Roman goddess, the personification of sensual pleasure. She was honored with a temple near the Porta Romanula (Romanula Gate). She was also called "Volupta."

❁ **ZELUS** was one of the sons of Styx and Oceanus. He was the dual personification of zeal, his positive aspect, and strife, his negative aspect.

❁ **ZEPHYRUS** was the god of the west wind. He was known as the mildest and gentlest of the four wind gods.

III

NYMPHS, DAEMONS & HYBRID CREATURES

❁ The **ALSEIDS** were a group of nymphs who lived in sacred groves in the woods.

❁ The **CENTAURS** were creatures that were half man and half horse. They were tempestuous and often violent. Two important exceptions were the Centaurs Cheiron, a teacher and healer, and Pholus.

❁ The three **CYCLOPES** were the third group of children born to Gaia and Uranus. Their names were Arges (Brightness), Brontes (Thunder) and Sterpes (Lightning).

❁ The **DACTYLS** lived on Mount Ida in Phrygia. Ten in number (five men and five women), they were believed to have been born through the ten fingers of Rhea as she grasped the Earth while giving birth to Zeus. The only ones whose names are certain are Acmon (anvil), Celmis (smelter) and Damnameneus (hammer). As their names suggest, they were credited with the discovery and working of iron.

❁ The three **FATES** determined the life span of each mortal being. Clotho spun the thread of life when the person was born; Lachesis measured a certain length; and Atropos cut the thread at the end of life. Even Zeus could not alter the will of the Fates.

❁ The three **FURIES** were Alecto (unresting), Megaera (jealous) and Tisiphone (avenger). They were born from the blood of Uranus after he was mutilated by Cronus. Known as the avenging goddesses, they relentlessly pursued Orestes after he murdered his mother, Clytemnestra, until he was acquitted by the Areopagus (Athenian council, presided by Athena). Their Greek name was the Erinyes.

❁ The twenty-four **GIANTS** were also born from the blood of Uranus, having the bodies of serpents and the heads of men. They rebelled against the Olympian gods and fought a war called the Gigantomachia. The Olympians finally won through their use of Herakles and his poisoned arrows. Alcyoneus and Porphyrion were the most prominent of the Giants; some of the others were Ephialtes, Euryptus, Clytius, Mimus, Enceladus, Polybotes, Gration, Argius and Thoas.

❁ The three **GORGONS** were Euryale, Stethno and Medusa, daughters of Phorcys (a sea god) and his sister Ceto. Medusa was the only one that was not immortal. She outraged Athena by violating one of her temples. Athena destroyed her beauty and then sent the hero Perseus to cut off her head.

❁ The three **GRACES** (or Charities) were Aglaea, Euphrosyne and Thaleia. They were daughters of Zeus and Eurynome.

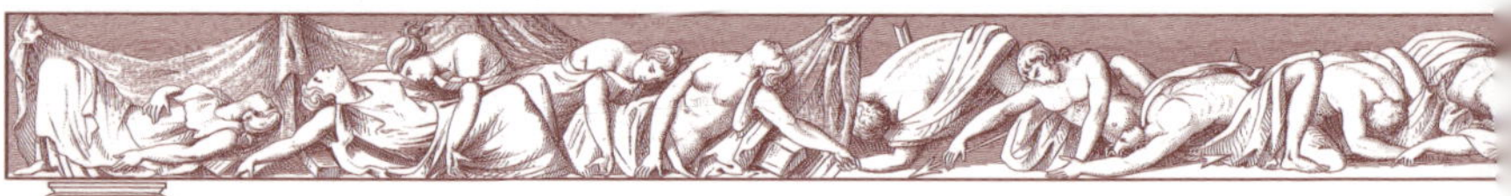

❁ The **GRAEAE** were three old, blind, toothless goddesses. Sisters to the Gorgons, their names were Dino, Enyo and Pemphredo. They shared one eye and one tooth and lived in a cave in the Atlas Mountains. Despite their poverty and loneliness, they were privileged to know all matters concerning the living. The Greek hero Perseus approached them and stole their one eye. He blackmailed them into telling him where the Gorgons resided and how to obtain the winged sandals, helmet and wallet that would allow him to reach the land of the Gorgons and slay Medusa.

❁ The **HAMADRYADS** were female wood nymphs connected to specific trees. They lived and died with the trees to which they were attached.

❁ The three **HARPIES**, Aello, Celaeno and Ocypete, were the winged daughters of Thaumus and Electra. Rapacious, bird-like women, they were instruments of divine vengeance.

❁ The three **HECATONCHEIRES** were the third group of the children of Uranus and Gaia, born after the Cyclopes. Known as Briareus, Cottus and Gyges, each had 100 huge arms.

❁ The three **HESPERIDES** were the daughters of Hesperus, the evening star. These three goddesses (Hespera, Aegle, Erytheis)

guarded the tree of golden apples that Gaia had given to Hera at the time of her wedding to Zeus. The eleventh labor of Herakles was to fetch the golden apples: he tricked the Titan Atlas into doing it for him.

❁ The **HORAE** (Hours) were the three nature goddesses who presided over weather and the change of seasons. Eunomia (Good Order), Dice (Justice) and Eirene (Peace) were their names. They were the daughters of Zeus and Themis.

❁ The **MELIADS** were nymphs of ash trees, born from the blood of Uranus, which fertilized Gaia.

❁ The **MUSES** were the nine daughters of Zeus and Mnemosyne (a Titanide), born through nine nights of love-making. Erato was the muse of Lyrics; Euterpe, of Music; Thalia, of Comedy; Melpomene, of Tragedy; Terpsichore, of Dance; Urania, of Astronomy; Clio, of History; Polyhymnia, of Hymns; and Calliope, of Epics.

❁ The **NAIADS** were water nymphs that inhabited springs, streams and fountains.

❁ The **NEREIDS** were water nymphs that lived in calm seas. It was believed they were fifty in number.

❁ The **OCEANIDS** were the children of Oceanus and Tethys. Although there may have been as many as 3,000 of them, the most important ones were Styx, Asia, Electra, Doris, Eurgnome and Metis.

❁ The seven **PLEIADES** were daughters of Atlas. Maia, Electra, Taygete, Celeno, Merope, Asterope and Alcyone supposedly became stars to avoid the passionate approaches of Orion, the great hunter. Their stars appear in the sky in late May.

❁ The **SATYRS** were half man and half goat. Inseparable from Dionysus, they pursued the Maenads and nymphs and represented the passionate (some would say decadent) forces of nature. Their parents may have been Hermes and Iphthima.

❁ The **SIRENS** were sea demons, half woman and half bird, the daughters of the river god Achelous. They lived on an island in the Mediterranean and sang so beautifully that sailors threw themselves overboard, as recorded in *The Odyssey*. Their names were Teles, Raedne, Molpe and Thelxiope.

❁ The twelve **TITANS** were the first group of children born to Gaia and Uranus. They were Oceanus, Tethys, Hyperion, Thea, Crius, Mnemosyne, Coeus, Phoebe, Iapetus, Themis, Cronus and Rhea.

IV

ON GODS & MORTALS

GENDER RELATIONS AMONG THE GODS

The twelve Titans derived their strength from their mother (Gaia) while the Olympians found their power in the thunderbolts of Zeus. This primordial conflict between the forces of earth and sky has many parallels in the myths of other peoples, but in few of them was the victory of the sky gods as clear as it was in the Greek world. After the war, Zeus and his fellow Olympians reigned from on high (Mount Olympus), while the forces of nature, represented by the Titans, were chained in Tartarus, the bowels of the earth.

Another clue to gender relations is seen in the relationship of Zeus and Hera. Zeus was a philanderer—something the Greeks mildly approved of—while Hera was shown as a shrew, a jealous woman, characteristics seen as worthy of contempt. Hera was probably an earlier Greek goddess of power and stature in her own right, who was transformed into the jealous wife depicted in the works of Homer and Hesiod. Thus it seems likely that the Greeks chose to honor the sky gods and masculine forces over those of the Earth gods and feminine powers. This may have occurred because they wanted to differentiate themselves from earlier, more "primitive," peoples like the Minoans.

WARFARE BETWEEN GODS & MORTALS

Few mortals tested the strength of the gods, but some heroes who did so escaped with their lives. Herakles was the most belligerent of the Greek heroes. He fought with Apollo, but was taken out of the fight by a thunderbolt thrown by Zeus. He wounded Hades, Hera and Ares in the battle for Pylos. He wrestled the river god Achelous and won his bride, Deianira. He fought at least twice with Ares and gained the upper hand both times. In fact, there seems to have been special antipathy between Ares and Herakles. The hero killed three of the god's mortal sons (Diomedes of Thrace, Cycnus and Lycaon) and stole the magic belt he had given to his daughter, Hippolyta, queen of the Amazons. Herakles's victories over Ares are attributed to both his greater wisdom (Ares was a wild and impetuous fighter) and the assistance given to him by Athena, who wanted to humiliate Ares, the god of war.

Diomedes fought and wounded both Ares and Aphrodite on the plain before Troy (helped by Athena, who wanted the Greeks to win the war). It seems safe to say that those heroes who fought against the gods did so at great peril and that without the assistance (overt or covert) of other gods, they would have been dispatched.

THE TROJAN WAR (The *Iliad*)

The Trojan War was fought between the Greek city-states and the city of Troy. The war began when Prince Paris of Troy stole Queen Helen of Sparta. For ten long years the Greeks fought on the open plain in front of Troy, which remained impervious to their attacks.

Hera and Athena, furious at Paris, were firmly on the side of the Greeks. Poseidon also favored the Greeks. Apollo favored the Trojans, as did Ares and Aphrodite. Zeus favored different sides at different times. Whether he actually loved either side is not known, because (unlike the lesser gods), he bowed to the will of the Fates. When his own mortal son came into danger, Zeus allowed him to be killed, knowing that no good could come of his attempt to intervene.

Many great and desperate battles were fought before Troy. In the absence of the Greek hero Achilles, Hector killed Patroclus. Roused from his torpor by this death, Achilles himself dispatched Hector outside the walls of Troy, before falling victim to an arrow in his ankle tendon. The Iliad ends with Hector's funeral, but Virgil's *Aeneid* preserved the story of the great hollow horse and the sack of Troy told in the lost "cyclic poems" of Greece. By this subterfuge, the Greeks gained access to the city and destroyed it. Helen was reclaimed by her husband, Menelaus.

THE WANDERINGS OF ODYSSEUS (The *Odyssey*)

Many Greek heroes reached home—only ten days' sail away—soon after the Trojan War was over, although some, including the great king of Mycenae, Agamemnon, came to bad ends. But the most troubled journey home was that of Odysseus, the clever and wily king of Ithaca (off the coast of Akarnania).

Odysseus provoked the anger of both Athena and Poseidon for outrages committed by the Greeks in their sack of Troy. He escaped alive from the terrific storm Athena sent to wreck the Greek ships on their way home, but Poseidon made certain that the voyage of Odysseus would take a very long time.

Odysseus and his small band of followers made their way around the Mediterranean in a disorganized, frenetic series of voyages, encountering one danger after another. He outwitted the giant Polyphemus, a son of Poseidon; escaped from the spells of Circe; and became the only man to claim he had heard the songs of the Sirens (he was tied down so that he could not jump overboard when he heard their singing). He spent years with the sea nymph Kalypso, who wanted to marry him and promised to grant him immortality if he would remain. Odysseus finally arrived in Ithaca a long, weary ten years after the fall of Troy. There he had to outwit many suitors for the hand of his ever-faithful wife, Penelope.

GREEK & ROMAN NAMES OF DIVINITIES

GREEK	ROMAN
Gaia	(Earth)
Uranus	(Sky)
Cronus	Saturn
Rhea	Ops
Zeus	Jupiter
Hera	Juno
Hestia	Hesta
Demeter	Ceres
Hades	Pluto
Poseidon	Neptune
Athena	Minerva
Persephone	Proserpina
Apollo	Phoebus
Artemis	Diana
Ares	Mars
Aphrodite	Venus
Hephaestus	Vulcan
Dionysus	Bacchus
Hermes	Mercury
Eros	Cupid
Pan	Faunus
Atlas	
Prometheus	
Herakles	Hercules